CHIMNEY & CO

THE POETIC STORY OF A FAMILY CAT

PAMELA DOUGLAS

CHIMNEY & CO.

© Pamela Douglas 2008

ISBN 978-1-906658-03-8

Chimney & Co. Illustrations by Pamela Douglas

Book Design, cover & Typesetting by;
David Stockman Creative Designer

Published by M-Y Books,
187 Ware Road,
Hertford.
m-ybooks.co.uk

To my family with love.

Chimney & Co.

FOREWORD 6

MY ARRIVAL 8

THE NAMING OF ME 10

MY LIFE SAVER 11

WHAT A FUNNY BLOKE 12

MY FRIENDS 15

SUSIE'S BEE 16

THE CHASE 18

NAUGHTY SUSIE 20

MY FIRST CHRISTMAS 28

SNOW 30

OH LOR! 31

CAT-CHAT 33

SUSIE IN RICHMOND PARK 34

MY FIELD MICE 36

TIME WASTING 38

PARTY PIECE 40

SUSIE – MOTHER 42

PRETENDING 43

MY FAVOURITE PERSON 44

TAKING MILK 46

THOSE PUPPIES 49

EVERYBODY OUT! 52

GROWING UP 55

BOATING LIFE 56

SADIE'S SORE PAW 59

BABY SPARROW 60

ALL PALS TOGETHER 62

GEORGE AND MRS. G 63

COUNTRY COTTAGE CAT 65

DREAMING 66

HELLO! 67

FUNNY FELLOW 70

VISIT TO THE VET 73

ON THE WINDOW- SILL 74

SUSIE AND SADIE 75

BREAKFAST IN THE GARDEN 76

JUST BECAUSE I'M ME 78

LEFT ALONE 80

THINKING 82

BRUSSELS SPROUTS 83

HIGH FLYING ME 85

THE WILLOW TREE 86

FOREWORD

She has a smudge upon her nose,

The beginnings of a frown,

Long stiff, white whiskers which,

When she is sad, droop tip-tilt down,

A soft white furry tummy

And, down the centre of her back,

A streak of darkest tabby,

All shades of brown and black,

Gentle, white plump paddy-paws,

Sharp ears, alert and keen,

A long black, beige-tinged handsome tail,

A lovely smile, her eyes are green.

She never looks untidy,

She has a character divine;

Do I think of her this way

Just because she's mine?

That was Chimney and this is her story....

Chimney & Co.

Chimney & Co,

MY ARRIVAL

One day a little girl,

Who was nearly four years old,

Came to choose an Irish Setter,

Who was ready to be sold.

My mother lived in kennels,

For dogs, not cats, you see,

And there, with lots of other kittens,

She had me.

The child picked Susie as

The pup she'd have that day,

Her parents were conversationing

In a boring grown-up way,

When she caught sight of all of us

In a box beneath a chair;

She was intrigued, she loved us all,

She decided then and there,

That I should be her kitten,

When I had grown to such a size

That I could leave my mother's caring

And had opened up my eyes.

Chimney & Co,

They arranged next time my owners
Were going near London Town,
They would parcel me most carefully
And take me travelling down.
So it was I came to make
That journey long and slow,
To end up labelled "TO BE CALLED FOR"
Down at Windsor's big Dog Show.

Chimney & Co,

THE NAMING OF ME

They chose the name of Chimney

That it should neither be

A male name nor a female,

It suited to a 'T',

For though I surely am, in truth,

The wrong sex for a She,

They looked at me and said I was

Too pretty for a He.

So that is why they speak of HER,

When really they mean HIM.

It does not worry me, of course,

For they usually call me Chim.

Chimney & Co,

MY LIFE SAVER

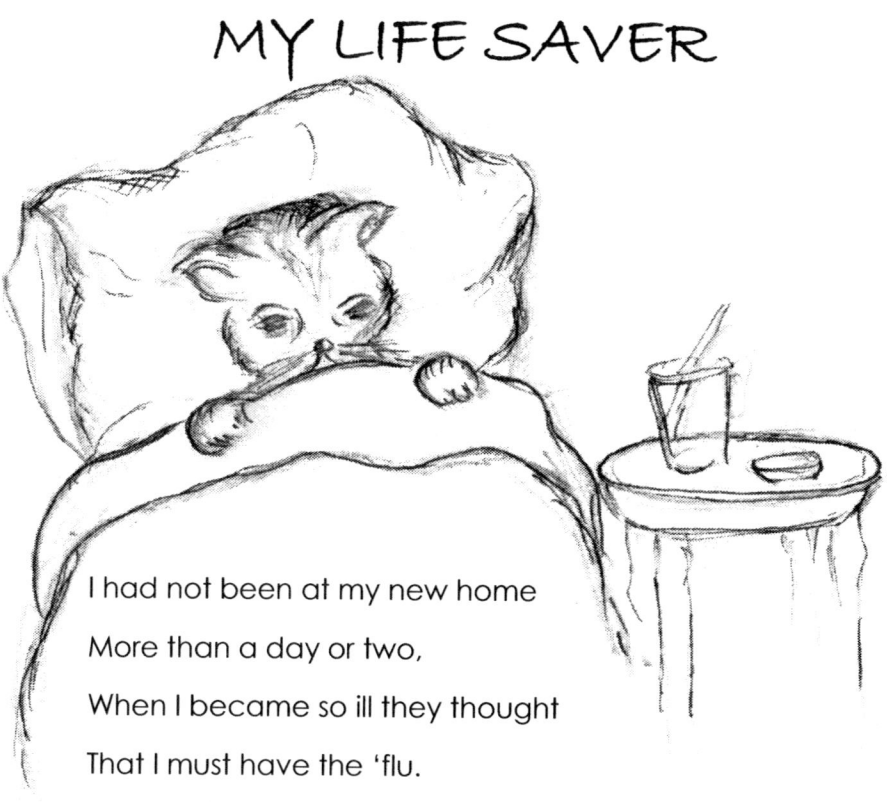

I had not been at my new home

More than a day or two,

When I became so ill they thought

That I must have the 'flu.

My nose would run, my eyes would stream,

I could not look at any cream;

I fell about, I scarce could stand,

I'd grown extremely thin,

They rushed me to the Vet, who filled

Me full of medicine.

And to that Vet I owe my life,

I was in such a state,

But for her expertise that night,

I now would be 'The Late'

WHAT A FUNNY BLOKE

Croak! Croak! Croak!

What a funny bloke;

His body seems to be on springs,

He nearly flies but has no wings.

Croak! Croak! Croak!

What a joke.

Perhaps he's cold, he has no coat,

It must be sore, his poor old throat.

Croak! Croak! Croak!

I wonder if he'd like a stroke.

Oh, goodness me, how odd he feels,

All cold and wet and clammy.

I don't suppose he has a name,

I think I'll call him Sammy.

Chimney & Co,

Croak! Croak! Croak!

He sounds as if he's going to choke.

I'll take him home and warm him there,

It's funny how he has no hair.

Croak! Croak! Croak!

What a comic bloke.

Croak! Croak! Croak!

Whoops!

What a joke.

Chimney & Co,

MY FRIENDS

There was Humphrey and Effie and Gambi,

There was Betsy and Teddy and Sue,

There was Nicholas, White Puss and Parla

And Mickey and Simon too.

There was Ursie and Humpty and Suki,

There was Jolly Wobble-eyes,

There was Emily, Quacker and Red Cat

And Dulcie, the doll who cries.

These were all the People

Who peopled the nursery.

One day, to all these People,

They added real live ME.

SUSIE'S BEE

Susie found a bumble bee,
One sunny summer's day,
A lovely buzzy bumble bee
Came flying by her way.

Susie was a puppy then,
She thought the bee was fun,
She felled it with one mighty paw,
She thought that she had won.

Chimney & Co,

Our Owner came into the room,

She dived towards the floor.

Gulp! That busy, buzzy bumble bee

Was no more.

Down to Susie's tummy

It buzzed and bizzed and sung,

It made a fight up to the last,

It stung her mouth and tongue.

That is why she's grown up

With this aversion to a buzz;

A fly, a wasp, mosquito, gnat

Annoy her, but I'm certain that

Of all the creatures that we see

She most cannot abide a bee.

THE CHASE

There was I in the garden,

It was a crisp Autumnal day,

The leaves were shining golden,

Caught in the sun's bright ray,

When down on to the pathway,

There ran a creature, whom

I had never seen before,

With a tail like a sweeping broom.

It sat down in the flower bed

And nibbled at a nut,

It scuttled up the trellis

And perched on the water butt.

I watched it for a moment,

I stalked across the grass,

It ran criss-cross before me,

It would not let me pass.

Chimney & Co,

It scampered up the Silver Birch

With me in hot pursuit,

It leapt from branch to branch,

It took a devious route.

I followed it from tree to tree,

I lost it in the bramble,

I'd never taken part before

In such a furious scramble.

Since that day I've learnt to live

In peace with these cheeky creatures;

So much so, they've now become

One of the garden's features.

Chimney & Co,

NAUGHTY SUSIE

Afternoon

Winter, cold

Puppy Susie

Nine months old

Walk on Heath

Mother, child

Off the lead

Running wild

Leap and bark

Having fun

Chasing leaves

Catching one.

Chimney & Co,

Other dogs

Roll and play

Going mad

Windy day

Call for home

Time to go

Puppy Susie

No! No! No!

Like it here

Don't want to go

Going home

No! No! No!

Run away

Round and round

Wont be caught

Go to ground

In the bushes

Out again

Hear them calling

Starts to rain

Will not come

Now they shout

Will not go back

Like to be out

Chimney & Co,

Raining hard

Soaking wet

Let them catch me

I'm their pet

Off I go

Don't want the lead

Calling, calling

Pay no heed

Pouring, blowing

Getting dark

See them going

Car Park..

Would they leave me

On my own?

Do not like it

All alone

Wait! I'm coming

Cars stream

This way, that way

Lights beam

Shiny road

Driving rain

Rushing out

Back again

Chimney & Co,

Tyres scream

Brakes screech

Where's the path?

Out of reach

Rush-hour traffic

Speeding wheels

Where to turn

Head reels

Jump aside

Now I see

Why I've a lead

Please rescue me.

Safely home

Muddy, wet

Kindly hands

Dry her and yet

That she's been bad

She's in no doubt

For a week

Not taken out

In the garden

Twice a day

Learn command

Stay!

And OBEY.

Chimney & Co,

Chimney & Co,

MY FIRST CHRISTMAS

Would you believe it ,

They've planted a tree,

There in the hallway,

Especially for me!

They've hung it with playthings

That sparkle and shine.

Can such a present

Really be mine?

But who else in this house

Would want such a thing

Who else plays with

Bells and ribbons and string?

No, it must be for me,

I'll give it a try.

There's a star on the top,

I wonder why.

Chimney & Co,

Those hanging toys,

What enormous fun,

I'll paw them off,

Every single one.

Now there just remains

The trunk to climb,

I'll soon reach the top,

That will take me no time.

CRASH! BANG!

Oh dear, dismay,

Everyone running.

What did they say?

How was I to know

It wasn't for me?

How was I to know

It was a Christmas Tree?

Chimney & Co,

SNOW

Good Heavens, what has happened to the world today?

The children all are shouting, "Hooray! Hooray!"

I do not recognise my garden as I look around,

A thick, white coverlet is hiding the ground.

Susie is out there rolling, jumping, eating,

I'm still curled up on the central heating.

Maybe I will try it, put my nose out of the door,

Carefully, gingerly, paw by paw.

Funny, it is soft, but oh, how cold!

Why have I never before been told

That suddenly my grass and my earth will disappear;

Does this always happen at this time of year?

Just look at the footprints I am making,

Funny what a long time I am taking

To get across the garden in this deep, soft foam,

This isn't a bit like my proper home.

This strange cold fluff is lining every tree

And look how white it is, it's whiter than me!

Chimney & Co,

OH LOR!

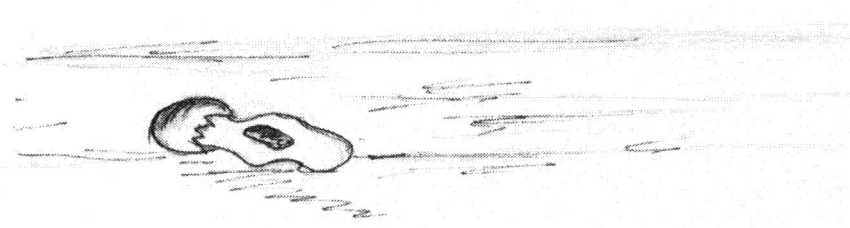

Have you ever noticed

What a lovely noise it makes

To stick your claws into an egg box

And how little time it takes

To send the contents crashing

Down to the polished floor?

Oh lor!

Chimney & Co.

CAT-CHAT

A new cat came to live next door;

He said to me one day,

"Do you ever get bored with the life you lead

And want to go away?"

"Good Gracious no, most certainly not!"

I said and told him that

I loved the kind of life I had,

For I was a Family cat.

"I'm glad to hear you utter thus,"

He said with olde worlde charm,

"I'm a similar sort of cat myself,

For I come from a farm.

But the thing I miss in urban streets

Is stopping for a chat."

So now, whenever we two meet,

We talk about this and that.

Chimney & Co,

SUSIE IN RICHMOND PARK

Susie's great love is for poodles

They were always her favourite breed;

Whenever she's met with a poodle,

They have instantly, promptly agreed.

So that Spring day she was taken to Richmond,

To the park where the deer run free,

Where the fluffy-tailed squirrels all scamper,

This is how she has told it to me.

At first, she could not believe it,

She could not believe her eyes,

As she saw all her fields were just covered

With poodles of every size.

There were grey ones and black ones

And small ones and fat ones,

They made a peculiar noise,

Not at all like her two cousin poodles,

Who had always been known as 'The Boys'.

Chimney & Co,

With a bound , she was right in amongst them,

Sending them leaping wide.

Not one would stay and play with her,

However hard she tried.

At last she had one parted,

All on its own and then,

As she pounced and wagged and sidled,

She was surrounded by angry men.

For what she had not known, was that

This roly-poly heap

Was not a playful poodle,

But a valuable sheep.

MY FIELD MICE

I found a family of field mice,

I said, "Would you like to see

What sort of a place I live in?

Come, come with me."

I took the tiniest field mouse,

He could not have been very old,

I carried him back to my house,

I said, "Now, you do as you're told.

Stay there while I fetch another,

All blue-grey furred and round-eared."

But when I returned to the kitchen,

The first one had disappeared.

Chimney & Co,

No matter, I thought, he's around,

I put Number Two on the floor,

I said, "You just stay where you are on the ground,

While I go back for more."

By the time I had gathered five field mice

And brought them all home, one by one,

I discovered why they had vanished,

I found out what had been done.

My owner had taken my party

And put them all in a box,

Had given them food and made them a nest

Out of scraps of old woollen socks.

And there she most carefully kept them,

I thought it an awful bore,

Until they were able to fend for themselves

And need be looked after no more.

Then she took them all on a journey,

One afternoon quite late,

She released them into the thicket

To live in their natural state.

TIME WASTING

I hate to see people working,

Working is no fun;

If I can stop someone working,

I feel a good job has been done.

I sit on every letter,

I lie on every book,

I jump up on the counter

Whenever someone starts to cook.

While my people sit a-sewing,

I paw off all the pins;

When the house is being painted,

I dabble in the tins.

Chimney & Co,

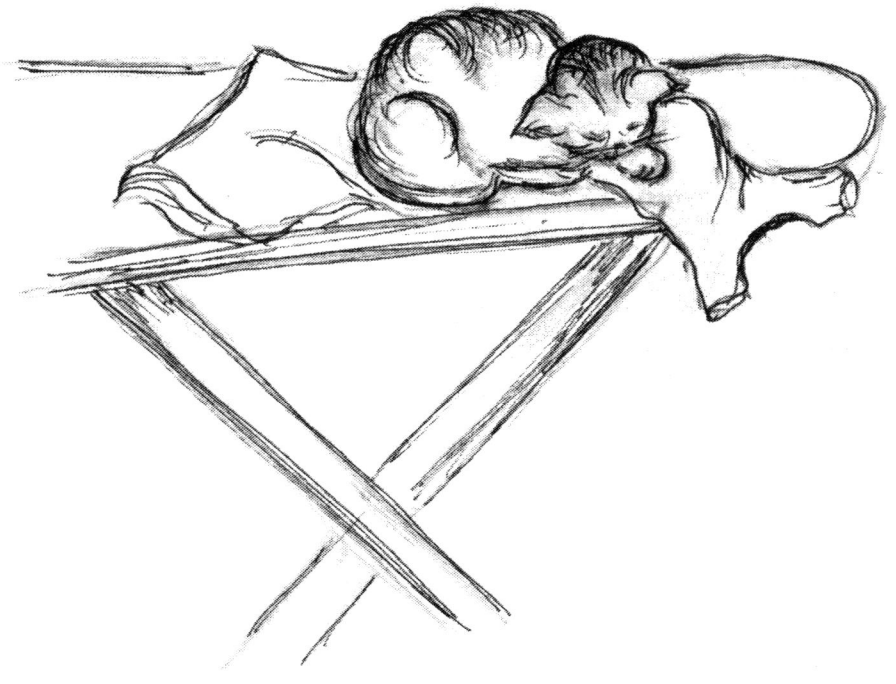

If anyone is ironing,

I try to pull the cord,

Then when the clean, washed clothes are spread,

I climb up on the board.

I love the daily papers,

I nibble at the news;

Whoever wants to waste their time

On other people's views?

Whoever wants to work all day,

When I am here to stroke and play?

Chimney & Co,   39

PARTY PIECE

My family gave a party,

A lovely bright affair,

With silver dishes on the table

And Champagne bubbles in the air.

The guests arrived in dozens,

Their cars all lined the street,

The house reverberated

To the sound of dancing feet.

Susie welcomed everybody

By standing at the door;

To all who stopped and spoke to her

She'd offer up her paw.

The garden all was floodlit,

It was a gorgeous sight,

The air was still, the flowers smelt sweet

On that warm, soft, summer night.

At about eleven thirty,

Susie said to me, "Come, quick!

It's just about the time that we

Should do our party trick.

Chimney & Co,

She found the centre spotlight,

She dragged me up the lawn,

My part in the act was simply

To pretend to being torn.

She took me by the collar,

She pulled this way and that,

The guests all shouted shrilly,

"What's that dog doing to that cat?"

But Susie's jaws were gentle,

She never held me tight,

We often used to play that game

To give our friends a fright.

Chimney & Co,   41

SUSIE – MOTHER

One puppy, two puppies, three puppies, four,

Five puppies, six puppies, seven puppies,

More?

Eight puppies, nine puppies, ten puppies,

No!

Yes, just one more tiny little puppy to go.

There they were eleven all told,

Soft and shiny and reddish gold;

Licked all over from head to toe,

Snuggling, squirming and wriggling so.

Proud Mother Susie, as pleased as could be,

Set them out for us all to see,

Then gathered them closely, warm and clean,

And settled for sleep, content and serene.

Chimney & Co,

PRETENDING

Sometimes I'm a door-stop,

Sometimes a china cat,

Sometimes a tea-cosy,

Like a great big furry hat.

Sometimes I'm a nightdress case,

Sometimes a weather vane,

For when I lie upon my head,

It means it's going to rain.

Sometimes I'm a wild cat,

A tiger or a lion,

Stalking through the undergrowth

With limbs of steel and nerves of iron.

Sometimes I'm a cuddle-puss

With soft and gentle paws,

Sometimes a paint remover

Scratching at the doors.

I'm not a bad footballer,

I dribble when I purr,

But the act I'm most renowned for

Is the shedding of white fur.

Chimney & Co,

MY FAVOURITE PERSON

He has music in his finger-tips
And laughter in his eyes,
He is gentle, kind and loving,
He is very old and wise.

When I know that he is coming,
I always sit just where,
As he comes in through the doorway,
He will find me waiting there.

Then I follow him about the house,
For I know a secret thing;
In his pocket he'll be carrying
A paper ball upon a string.

He always seems to find the time
To treat me to a game;
On each and every visit
He is always just the same.

I love him and he loves me too,
I think it must be sad
For families who do not know
The joy of a Granddad.

Chimney & Co,

Chimney & Co,

TAKING MILK

I always take my milk from a tray,
I would not have it any other way;
I could not drink it from the floor,
Whatever do they take me for?
No, I always take my milk from a tray.

In the morning, when my owners
Have their breakfast up in bed,
There am I a-purring,
Whiskers straight and pert my head,
Until they pour that saucer full
Of creamy milk and say,
"There you are now Chimney,
There's your milk upon the tray."

At tea-time in the afternoon,

I hear the cups a-clatter,

I come seemingly from nowhere,

All my paws a pitter-patter,

And sit upon the sofa

In my special sort of way,

Until they pour my milk

Into a saucer on the tray.

Chimney & Co,

THOSE PUPPIES

Those puppies,

How they did grow.

Those puppies,

How they did eat.

Those puppies,

How they did love to nibble human ears and feet.

Those puppies,

How they did fight.

Those puppies,

How they did play.

Those puppies,

How they did stop their games and fall asleep half-way.

Those puppies,

How Susie loved

Those puppies,

How they loved her.

Those puppies,

How soft and warm, dressed in their shiny, red-gold fur.

Those puppies,

How they did squeal.

Those puppies,

How they'd escape.

Those puppies,

How well and truly Susie licked them into shape.

Those puppies,

There came the day,

Those puppies

Nearly all were gone.

Those puppies,

We said Goodbye to all those puppies save for one.

That puppy

Is with us now.

That puppy,

What a mischievous lady.

That puppy

Is ours to keep and love, they have named that puppy

SADIE.

Chimney & Co,

EVERYBODY OUT!

Suddenly the lights go out,

It is a CUT they say.

A CUT the cake, a CUT of meat?

It does not come my way.

         I watch the candles splutter,

         It is a STRIKE I find.

         A STRIKE the gong, a STRIKE a match?

         It does not seem that kind.

Now I gradually remember,

Way back a year ago,

January or December,

Our lights kept going low.

         This year it is the Miners,

         Last year the Power Men,

         And only just the year before

         Our rubbish piled up by the door,

         It was the Dustmen then.

Who will be the next to go,

The Railways or the Gas,

The Buses or the Airlines,

The postmen out en masse?

Chimney & Co,

It seems to be the fashion,

These days, to make a row,

No matter who will suffer,

They'll get their way somehow.

So come on all you felines,

Unite to fight with tooth and claw,

Let us march up to Trafalgar Square,

A banner in each paw.

There we'll demand the Government

Should pass a new law that,

Each Friday they will hand out

A free mouse to every cat.

Chimney & Co,

Chimney & Co,

GROWING UP

When Susie was a puppy,

I was a kitten too,

So I did not take much notice

Of the changes she went through;

Of her long and lanky puppy legs,

Her thin and scraggy tail,

Of her sharp, white teeth and bouncy run,

That look of mischief, when she'd done

Some extra special wicked deed,

Like chewing up the chair, or burying her lead.

But now that I am all of four

And Sadie is but one,

I can see how she has grown,

Has changed her coat to a darker tone,

Has silken feathers flowing down

Her sturdy legs, has lost her frown.

She's still a heap of fun at play,

But has developed in some way

A character all of her own,

So when we see her with her mother,

We'll not mistake one for the other.

BOATING LIFE

I don't often go on a journey,

But I seem to be going today,

The car is loaded with luggage,

Could we all be going away?

The dogs are both here with their leads on,

Two children excitedly talk,

I do sometimes go for a ride to the park,

But this is surely more than a walk.

Several hours and many miles later,

I find out what it's all been about.

We've arrived, unpacked all our luggage,

I'm awoken and   taken out.

Chimney & Co,

There's a boat standing by the embankment,

There are cabins and bunks and a wheel.

I gingerly try out the cat-walk

To see if I'll get the feel.

The engine starts up, we are moving,

I retire to a nook in the bow,

And there do I stay for the rest of the day,

Not a sound, not a squeak, not a miaow.

The movement, at last, has abated,

I peep out for a quick look around.

I make up my mind that I'll spend all the night

Leaping backwards and forwards to ground.

For the rest of the trip we all manage

So to organise everyone right,

The children and dogs in command for the day

And I am on watch through the night.

Chimney & Co,

SADIE'S SORE PAW

Sadie has always loved her walks
In the fresh, wild open air,
But she came back in pain one day,
She had hurt her paw out there.

She had run so happily
Across the soft, spring grass,
When suddenly her paw fell on
A jagged piece of glass.

She limped, she whimpered as that paw
Was dressed and bound up tight.
I tried to comfort her with purrs,
She whimpered through the night.

How easy it would be to put
A piece of glass or tin
Into a safe container,
To put it in a bin.

But humans do not seem to care,
As they hurl their rubbish wide,
They do not think of the pain they cause
As they litter the countryside.

Chimney & Co,

BABY SPARROW

I caught a baby sparrow

And I brought my baby sparrow

Straight back into the house for all to see;

But they took my baby sparrow

And they nursed my baby sparrow,

They took my baby sparrow right away from me.

They fed my baby sparrow

And they flew my baby sparrow,

He sat there twittering as happy as could be.

We watched my baby sparrow,

We sat and eyed my baby sparrow,

All of us, Susie, Sadie and me.

They loved my baby sparrow,

He grew tame, my baby sparrow,

All their friends came round and made the greatest fuss.

As we listened to that sparrow,

We came to loathe my baby sparrow,

It seemed they loved that baby sparrow more than us.

Chimney & Co,

He grew well, my baby sparrow,

They released my baby sparrow,

He flew off across the garden, strong and free.

They waved Goodbye to baby sparrow,

They wished him luck, my baby sparrow,

That's the last time I bring a baby sparrow home to tea.

ALL PALS TOGETHER

The dogs are very good to me,

They let me eat their food,

I walk right underneath them to their plate;

They let me have first pickings

Before they join in too,

They stand aside and wait if I am late.

I drink out of their water bowl,

I lie upon their beds,

And when you think I am but the size of their two heads,

They could well and truly overpower me,

With one gulp devour me,

Especially as I never show a claw.

I never scratch or hiss at them,

If ever I am mad at them,

We quickly make it up and shake a paw.

Yes, they are very good to me,

I'm glad I'm understood to be

On equal terms with such a pair;

For we respect each other,

Have great love for one another,

So there's hardly anything that we don't share.

Chimney & Co,

GEORGE AND MRS. G

My family sometimes go away,
We know the signs to look for,
Busy rushing round the house,
Bags and cases on the floor;
But we need not be unhappy,
For they've promised us, you see,
They'll always leave us in the care
Of George and Mrs. G.

When they holiday in England,
They always take us too,
At the seaside, in the country,
We know just what to do;
But when they go abroad they can't,
There's quarantine, you see,
And so they leave us in the care
Of George and Mrs. G.

Although we miss them greatly
And long for their return,
Are sad to see them driving off,
We now have come to learn
That we shall not be lonely,
For they've promised us, you see,
They'll always leave us in the care
Of George and Mrs. G.

We need not fear the kennels
Or a stranger's voice or touch,
We need not eat some odd new food
We do not care for much;
We are indeed so lucky,
For they've promised us, you see,
They'll not leave us with anyone
But George and Mrs. G.

Chimney & Co,

COUNTRY COTTAGE CAT

I hear we'll soon be moving

To a country home and that

I must practice being

A Country Cottage Cat.

It wont be hard for me, of course,

I've lots of country ways,

I love sitting in the window

With a dreamy, far-off gaze.

At the moment, I'm inventing

A country pose upon the mat

And people passing point and say,

"Look at that   Country Cottage Cat!"

So, if you catch me sniffing flowers

In a knowing sort of way,

Or intimating that the sweet-corn

Would be better left a day,

You will know I'm just rehearsing

And making certain that,

When I get there, I will be a

Proper Country Cottage Cat.

Chimney & Co,   65

DREAMING

I'm sitting in the apple tree,

It's a crab-apple tree in fact,

The time is Spring, the sky is blue,

All the blossom is still intact,

A tiny cloud of cotton wool

Is hanging in the air;

I wonder as I gaze at it,

Who left it there?

Chimney & Co,

HELLO!

I was lying in my basket
As they came through the door.
"Hello!" I said,
Each turned their head,
"Did you hear that?
A talking cat!"
I'd learnt the word, of course,
Some time before.

I'd never tried it out until
That very day, I chose
To speak the word
They'd never heard
Come from a cat,
Straight out like that,
Then from my basket,
Languidly, I rose.

Now nobody believes them
When they say they've heard me speak,
No-one believes,
Without their seeing,
That I spoke like
A human being.
I'll try it out again
One day next week

SEASIDE HOLIDAY

We all went to the coast one year,

To a cottage by the sea;

The air was clean, it smelt of salt,

The wind blew fresh and free.

The dogs enjoyed their romping

By the shore, the sea, the sand,

My paws preferred to stay at home

On more familiar land.

There came to mar the beauty of a breezy summer day,

The sight of Susie, black from tail to head,

Every whisker, every hair,

Thick black slime was clinging there,

It was tar, it was oil they said.

Chimney & Co,

As all hands set to clean her

With olive oil and such,

I thought of all those seagulls,

Though I'd never liked them much;

I wondered what they'd do

If they ever got in such a state,

How would they fly,

Or would they die,

Or would they simply wait

And hope someone would find them

Before it was too late.

I learnt a lot, that year, about pollution,

I thought that much of it was caused by human greed;

What possibly could be a sane solution

In this so-called enlightened life we lead?

Always somebody, it seems, can make more money

Out of destruction, out of ruin, out of pain;

In the preservation of this planet's natural beauty

There is not such opportunity for gain.

Each and every one is so affected,

Children, men and women, creatures too,

For looking round the world now-a-days, you sadly see

The only safe place for my own wild kind to be

Is in a private park or in a zoo.

Chimney & Co,

FUNNY FELLOW

It was a cold and wet November night

I met this little fellow,

He said he was a Hamster,

He was a sort of golden yellow.

He had thick soft fur,

But had no tail,

His tiny pale, pink paws

Looked frail.

"What are you doing," I said to him,

"Out in this sort of weather?"

"I think I'm lost," he answered me,

"I'm sure I'm where I should not be,

Shall we walk together?"

Chimney & Co,

"By all means," so said I to him,

"But if you do not mind,

Come back home with me instead,

It's warmer there you'll find."

And so it was I guided him

Through my private door,

Straight across the kitchen,

Out to the hallway floor

Once there, to my amazement,

He ran to the furthest wall

And, sitting up behind a boot,

Let out a rasping call.

The family came running

And grabbed my new found friend;

Our freshly formed acquaintanceship,

It seemed, was at an end.

I was not entirely sorry,

He would be no good for play,

He said he was nocturnal,

He was not lively in the day.

They hung him in the bird cage,

Fed him food he never ate,

All he seemed to want to do

Was to hibernate.

Chimney & Co,

Chimney & Co,

VISIT TO THE VET

I woke up that morning with a very sore paw,

I could not put it firmly on the ground,

It was just a little swollen,

It was tender, it was raw,

It was most incapacitating I found.

The Vet would know the remedy,

She always had before,

You only had to go to her

And show her your bad paw,

For her to have it better

In the twinkling of an eye;

She'd not only know that it was hurting,

She would also tell you why.

But this morning, on our visit,

We saw a different face,

There seemed something was different,

It seemed a different sort of place.

It appeared she was not attending to her animals that day,

Someone else had taken over, she had gone away.

Later on, with sadness, I learned the truth,

That she had died.

I cried.

ON THE WINDOW-SILL

I love to sit on the window-sill
And watch the world go by,
I love to sit on the window-sill
And blink up at the sky,
I love to sit on the window-sill
And gaze at the Hornbeam tree,
I watch the pigeons nesting there
And staring back at me.

I love to sit on the window-sill
And watch the rain beat down,
I love to sit on the window-sill
And see the leaves turn brown,
I love to sit on the window-sill
And feel the warmth around,
When winter snow comes falling
And covers up the ground.

Chimney & Co,

SUSIE AND SADIE

How would you describe an Irish Setter,

How would I, a cat, describe mine?

What choice of words would be the better

Their nature to define?

Loving, gentle, faithful,

Beautiful we know,

Fun, vivacious, playful,

Soft brown eyes, a noble head they show;

But perhaps the word that most immediately

Springs into my mind,

That colours all their qualities,

Is that they are kind,

So very kind.

BREAKFAST IN THE GARDEN

There's a big round table in the garden,
Where summer meals are spread,
But in the long, cold winter
Robin breakfasts there instead.

The blue-tits and the sparrows
Hang upside down, like acrobats,
On the food container,
Hung safely high away from CATS..

But Robin cannot cling
On to the wire mesh there,
So he comes hop-hop-hopping
To the table for his fare.

I sit underneath the table
And watch them all fly by,
Two chaffinches come sometimes,
They don't stay long, they're rather shy.

In the morning early,
Squirrel comes to eat his fill;
He tries to steal the coconut,
One day he will.

Chimney & Co,

I would not harm these birds because
My family love them true,
If I hurt one, it would hurt them
And that I will not do.

No, I just sit and study them,
I sit and contemplate,
I watch their every movement,
I sit and watch and wait.

Chimney & Co,

JUST BECAUSE I'M ME

I suppose I am most dreadfully spoilt,

For example, when it is wet,

The dogs have to sit on the mat and be dried,

Each paw separately and yet,

I can come in through the flap in my door

And leave a trail all over the floor

Of the muddiest paw-marks you ever did see,

Just because I'm ME.

Then again, the dogs are not allowed on chairs,

But I lie around on them, leaving my hairs

All over the cushions as you can see,

Just because I'm ME.

A tea-time, I always take my milk

From a saucer on the tray;

If the dogs put their noses so close to the food,

They are told to go away,

But all I do if I feel like a drink

Is climb up on my owner's knee,

Just because I'm ME.

Chimney & Co,

When the dogs are taken up the road,

They have to wear a lead,

But I pop out whenever I like

And no-one pays any heed.

It's the same at night when we're put to bed,

The dogs are locked in when goodnights have been said,

But I'm allowed in and out as late as can be,

Just because I'm ME.

You might think that all these favours

Would cause friction between us three,

But the dogs seem to take it for granted.

Why?

Just because I'm ME

LEFT ALONE

Sometimes the house is terribly quiet,

Nobody is about.

I pad through the house and nothing stirs,

Everyone is out.

A dress hangs limply on a chair,

A half-read paper strewn

Across the table,

I hope they come back soon.

Food is there upon my plate,

Fresh water in my bowl,

I don't think I am hungry,

There is not another living soul,

It seems, for miles and miles around;

It is a strange uncanny feel,

It's as if the house is imitation

And I'm the only one who's real.

Chimney & Co,

Then suddenly there's life again,

There's fun and joy and sound,

There is laughter, there is movement,

There are tails a-wagging round.

All my people have returned to me,

I'll not be lonely any more;

Is it really true they left

Less than one hour before?

THINKING

We just go on living, seeing, breathing,

We just go on living,

I wonder why.

We just go on eating, drinking, sleeping,

We just go on living,

Why don't we die?

We just go on running, barking, miaowing,

We just go on living,

Sometimes we cry.

We just go on wagging, purring, loving,

Of course,

We just go on loving,

And being loved,

That's why.

BRUSSELS SPROUTS

There is nothing I like better

Than playing football with a sprout,

A Brussels Sprout.

I remember them from year to year

And whenever those funny little cabbages appear,

I'm up there on the sink to fish one out,

A Brussels Sprout.

I then knock it off on to the ground

And chase it round

And round

And round.

I never eat it, what a thought!

Though some, I suppose, would say I ought;

But I do get irritated

When, after I have waited

For my especial sprout to be prepared,

That the dogs should come and claim it,

Cart it off and roughly maim it,

Break it up

And leave it in a thousand pieces there.

Not fair.

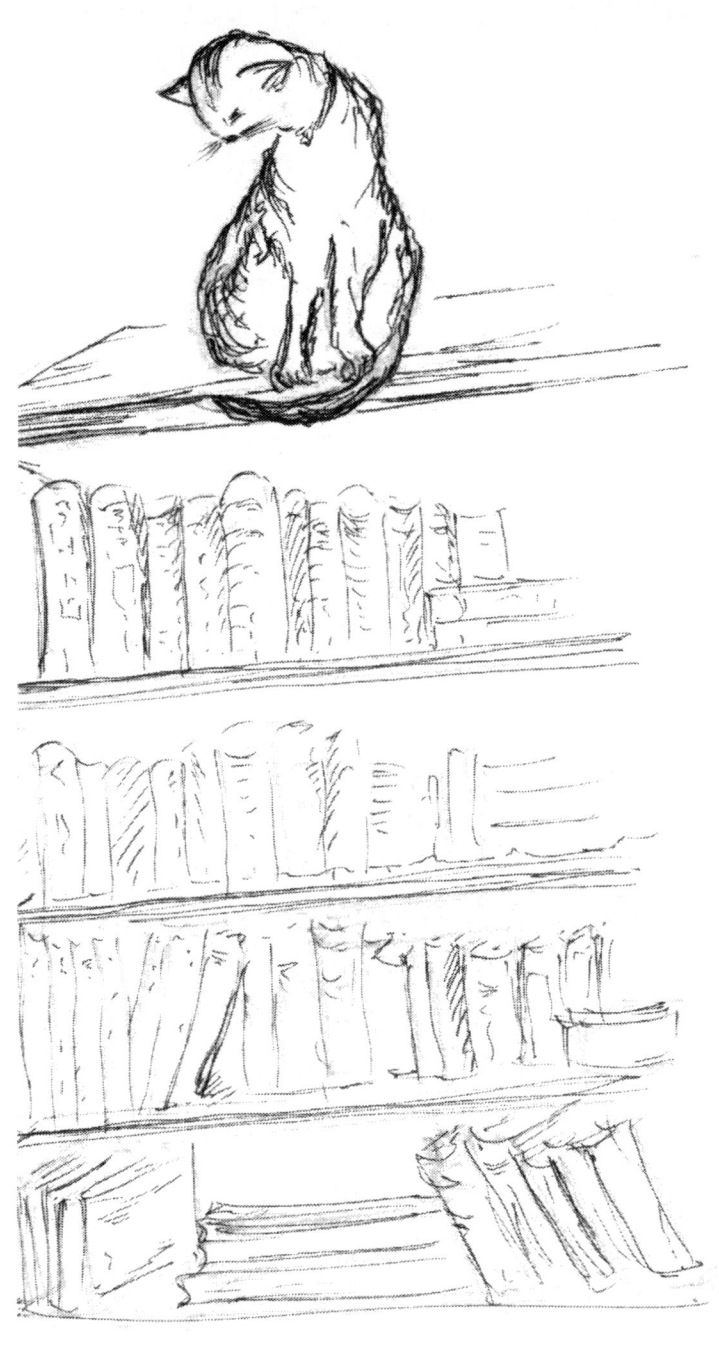

Chimney & Co,

HIGH FLYING ME

I've become a sitting-up cat,

A sitting-up on THINGS,

On tables, desks and work-tops,

It's as if I've just grown wings

That take me flying upwards

On chests of drawers and chairs,

Could the reason be that now

We haven't any stairs?

Every time you find me

Taking forty winks or so,

You will be sure to see me lying

A few feet above your toe.

It's not that there's a draft about,

I really can't think why

I've suddenly this urge to be

Permanently high.

THE WILLOW TREE

At the beginning of September,

Several years back now,

We said farewell to Susie,

I miaowed a farewell miaow.

How sad we were that Autumn,

For we loved her so, you see,

How we cried as she was laid to rest

Beneath the Willow Tree.

We remembered how her tail had thumped

In joy and welcome true,

How gentle, loving, faithful

She had been her whole life through.

Sadie missed her most perhaps,

For she had never known

A life without her mother,

She had never been alone.

Although we tried to comfort her,

We could not take the place

Of lovely, gentle Susie,

Of her gentle, lovely face.

Chimney & Co,

Now Sadie, too, has taken leave,

Perhaps she's glad that she

Can join her mother once again

Beneath the Willow Tree.

I often stroll beyond the lawn

And visit that twin grassy mound,

I think how peaceful it must be

To lie asleep, deep underground.

I feel so grateful I've been spared

To stay a while and give a fuss

To those who, throughout the years,

Have loved and cherished all of us.

And when I die, I'll go in peace,

For they have promised me

They'll gently lay me down to rest

Beneath that dear old Willow Tree.

Chimney & Co,

Authors appreciation and thanks to those who helped along
the way.
To Jonathan of M-Y Books for having faith,
To David for transposing my ideas in his own artistic way and
to my loyal home team, Louise and Hannah for their constant
love and support.

Chimney & Co,

Other books by Pamela Douglas

HYAM
The Cat Who Talked Too Much

ISBN 978-1-906658-13-7

ANIMALS IN MY LIFE

ISBN 978-1-906658-16-8

THE WHO'S AFRAID STORIES

ISBN 978-1-906658-15-1

Pamela's books are also available as audiobooks, read by the author. For more information please visit the M-Y Books website:- **m-ybooks.co.uk**

Chimney & Co,